MEGA MONSTERS

Timothy Kane

TRIUMPH
BOOKS

This book is available in quantity at special discounts for your group or organization. For further information, contact:
Triumph Books
542 South Dearborn Street
Suite 750
Chicago, Illinois 60605
(312) 939-3330
Fax (312) 663-3557
www.triumphbooks.com

Printed in U.S.A.
ISBN: 978-1-60078-512-2

Design and page production by Andrew Burwell

MEGA MONSTERS

MEGA MONSTERS

THE WORLD OF MONSTER TRUCKS

From the name "monster truck," you can imagine that a lightning bolt hit a pile of debris in a junkyard somewhere in Transylvania. The electric spark spawned the first giant-wheeled pickup and it burst out from under some moonlit scrap heap. The truck's sole purpose was to churn up mud and run over the rusting hulks of less worthy vehicles.

Early builders of monster trucks were like Dr. Frankenstein. These gearhead hobbyists were modern day mad doctors. They went into junkyards looking for donors the same way Dr. Frankenstein and his stooge, Igor, went to cemeteries looking for bodies.

Dr. Frankenstein wanted to construct a large, powerfully built man, who was super-smart and super-strong. He used assorted body parts, all powered by a lightning bolt. He

messed up when he couldn't find the right kind of brain. And, as everyone knows, Frankenstein's monster went crazy and wrecked the doctor's laboratory.

Just like Dr. Frankenstein, monster truck builders were trying to build a super truck. Instead of a brain, they went looking for big wheels – like those used on tractors on farms. They are the telltale features of any monster truck. If you were to describe the Frankenstein monster, you would describe the heavy shoes, high forehead and bolts in the neck. In the same way, a monster truck

BOUNTY
HUNTER

Owner:	CSK Auto Corporation
Style:	Ford Expedition
Engine:	555 Blown Alcohol
Home:	Tonganoxie, Kansas
Created:	2003
Source:	www.offroaders.com

has similar features – it's a snorting pickup with humongous wheels.

The big wheels with giant treads allow the monsters to climb out of ruts, swamps, mud pits, valleys and canyons. Monster truck adventures take them down into the murkiest lowlands and up onto the highest mountaintops – places that would have swallowed up and defeated weaker vehicles. Many off-road drivers of monsters refuse to wash off the mud splattered onto their vehicles after slimy journeys. Dirt is a badge of honor.

Monster trucks start out as modified four-wheel-drive pickups. Nothing can stop a gearhead's desire to tinker with a V8 engine, juicing up its power and giving it

the ability to drive over uneven landscapes. In time, large engines, heavy-duty suspension and large wheels were added to make monster trucks more powerful, more mobile and more menacing.

In the old days of the sport – back in the 1970s and 1980s – big-bodied pickups that had an engine compartment with enough room for a supercharged V8 engine were needed. The bodies of big, American-made four-wheel-drive pickups – like Ford, Dodge and GM – were the most desirable because they had an engine compartment where a monster-big engine can fit.

For today's monster maker bent on creating a car crusher, finding the truck body is just the beginning when bringing a monster

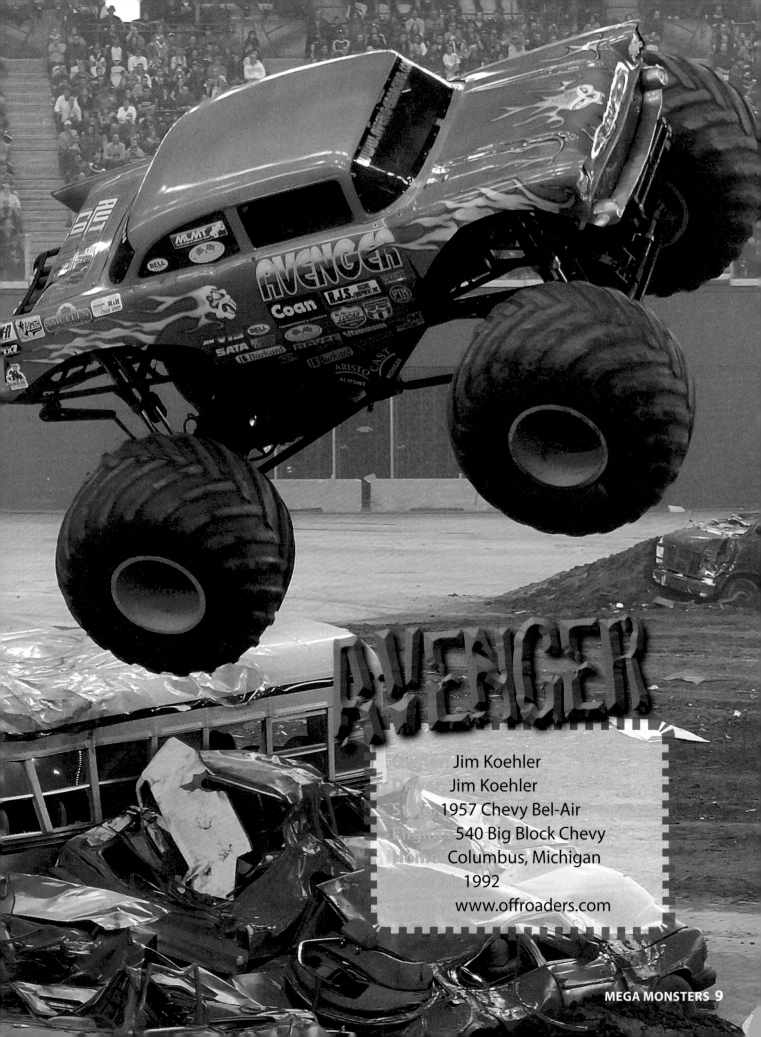

Jim Koehler
Jim Koehler
1957 Chevy Bel-Air
540 Big Block Chevy
Columbus, Michigan
1992
www.offroaders.com

to life. You have to get parts that work well together. Some welding, sawing, hammering and drilling may be necessary. Many hours will be spent in the garage-laboratory.

You'll also need to find a super-charged engine and sturdy transmission with a lower gear ratio that can handle the powerful torque that will enable the monster to stand up on its rear wheels, like a doggy asking for a treat. You'll also need longer and sturdier drive shafts.

The brain of a monster truck is the driver. He or she needs to be smart – mechanically inclined to know what the monster can do and what it can't. The driver has to be tough and competitive. The driver must enjoy danger. Jumping over a school bus or a pit of burning tar is not for the weak-kneed. Monster trucks are also expensive and can cost as much as a

house. Many young drivers cannot afford to own a monster truck, so they drive one for somebody else. They scan newspapers and go online looking for ads that say: "Wanted, Monster Truck Driver."

Roll bars are also needed to protect the driver. All modern monsters have automatic turn-off switches that shut off the flow of fuel when trucks roll over, as they often do. Drivers need to wear helmets and racing harnesses.

THE HISTORY OF MONSTER TRUCKS

The history of monster trucks begins in the 1970s, when car mechanics started tinkering with their American-made four-wheel-drive pickup trucks. These fans decided they wanted to modify their trucks and prepare them for punishing conditions and acts of unspeakable cruelty.

They wanted to test the limits of their vehicles, and not even the Edsel – Ford's most-famous lemon, which has come to epitomize failure – deserved to be crushed in such a manner. The transition began with fitting the trucks with large tires. The big tires would come first and the remainder would be built from the axle up.

The man regarded as the father of the monster-truck phenomenon is Bob Chandler from St. Louis. He reportedly invented

the first monster truck. He constructed a monster he nicknamed "BIGFOOT." Truck-a-Rama promoter Bob George saw BIGFOOT and called it a "monster truck" in 1980. He gets the credit for the naming the sport.

BIGFOOT first crushed a car in April of 1981 – and started the crowd-pleasing destruction craze. This historic event was

captured on film and can still be seen on YouTube. Chandler was working as a carpenter at the time. He must have come from a job because you can see the lumber bouncing around in BIGFOOT's cargo bed during the experience. The BIGFOOT monster mounts and crushes two cars. Their roofs cave in, the windshields collapse and the headlights burst. BIGFOOT claimed the glory on this day. The first two victims were muscle cars. The two vehicles were flattened and disgraced. Their makes, models and years were not recorded, as there is no glory for the conquered.

A promoter saw the historic first-crush film and invited Chandler to run over cars in front of live audiences. Chandler performed in small shows, leading to the biggest event yet at the Pontiac Silverdome in 1982, This sparked major interest when BIGFOOT was joined by a number of other trucks on tour, including Bear Foot and King Kong.

In 1985, the U.S. Hot Rod Association and TNT Motorsports began to race the monsters,

MEGA MONSTERS

which changed their design. They had to become lighter to become faster. Many monsters were fitted with fiberglass bodies. The Monster Truck Racing Association was established in 1988 to create rules to improve safety. Other monsters with scary names emerged.

Throughout the 1990s, freestyle shows became popular. Watching a freestyle monster truck event is like watching a dance competition. The trucks rear up on their back tires, thunder around the track and jump over flaming jumbo jets. Other monster truck organizations emerged, including Monster Jam in 1995, and its most famous fiend – Grave Digger.

A TALE OF TWO MONSTERS

Years ago, monster trucks had two lives. Their first years were spent, for example, as a regular pickup truck sitting on the lot of

a Ford or Chevy dealership. A construction worker buys it to haul his tools. Next, a grandmother, looking for a secondhand vehicle, buys it from the worker and now it hauls groceries. Later, she leaves it in her will to her teenage grandson, who uses it to get to school. Time passes. The grandson becomes a man. As the years go by, the pickup ages and rusts. The radio stops working. The gift from granny starts burning oil and belching smoke. One day it conks out. It would be cheaper to junk the pickup than to pay to have the engine replaced. So off it goes into retirement.

Once a truck is abandoned, it gets hauled off to the junkyard, the resting place for rusting hulks. Somebody comes by and pries off the chrome emblem. Now the truck is nameless. One day, with a change of luck, a mechanic finds it. He resuscitates the wreck. He gives it the kind of life that none of its past drivers ever dreamed possible.

MEGA MONSTERS

The gearhead puts in a bigger engine, bigger suspension and bigger wheels. In its second life – the life of a monster – it can now climb cliffs, wallow in the mud or race along the beach as the tide comes in.

That was the old way. There is no boring first life for the newest generation of monsters. They skip the larva stage and become a butterfly straightaway. The first time their engine turns over, these monsters are ready to climb sand dunes. They are designed in a lab by experts using computers, and are built from scratch, with no possibility that they can be anything else but monsters. The newest generation have skeletons of steel tube. At first, the pros tried to use aluminum tube, but aluminum was too weak for performing. The punishing show circuit requires these trucks to race, jump over school buses and do back-flips off of dirt ramps.

The skin of a stadium monster is made of fiberglass. When it does a flip and lands upside down, the fiberglass body cracks apart and is swept up. There is no need to hire a body shop man to do a facelift and fix the dents. These skins on the newer monsters are totally replaceable. The fiberglass of a modern monster comes off just as easy as a Halloween mask – they are just as scary and colorful too.

THE EVOLUTION OF MONSTERS

Things that slither from the primordial soup don't stay the same, they evolve. They learn to live on land, they grow feet, they get bigger.

Evolution for monster trucks means they get meaner and more destructive. Just like Godzilla, who walks down the street, picking up buses, shoving trains off their tracks and crushing taxicabs along the way, four-wheeled monsters do their own crushing.

Take, for example, the tale of Robosaurus, self-described as the world's tallest robot.

It's the brainchild of monster makers who wanted to turn a toy into a real-life monster. They were inspired by Transformers. Those innocent-looking toys may only look like a truck or a car, but can sprout arms and legs and sharp teeth in a moment's notice.

Size and scope are part of a kid's imagination. To a kid, a Transformer is a humongous beast who can kick out the wall of a Lego house, scatter a Lincoln Log fence or destroy G.I. Joe's camp in a matter of moments. However, when it comes to the real thing, Robosaurus can impress any young mind.

A performance with Robosaurus starts with its arrival at the event – usually a county fair or a stock-car race. It begins as a nice little package. Towed in by a semi-tractor truck, the trailer looks as if it could be a delivery of California tomatoes. It seems like any old vehicle, but that's not right. Something is peculiar about this container. The trailer starts groaning. It unfolds. It sprouts a head and claws. Once upright, it picks up and eats unsuspecting sedans and pickup trucks. Their fuel tanks explode. Robosaurus has also been seen eating air force fighter jets.

By comparison, Robosaurus dwarfs the real prehistoric dinosaur Tyrannosaurus Rex. T. Rex was only 15 feet tall, but Robosaurus is nearly 50 feet tall, weighs about 30 tons and snorts flames and plumes of black smoke out of nostrils the size of manholes. Parents recoil in fear at their first glimpse of this mechanical beast. Did they make a mistake bringing their children here? They're ready to run for their lives, but the kids encourage them to stick around and enjoy the show.

The brain of Robosaurus is a very human-looking person known as Mark Hays. He is the president of Monster Robot Inc. and is Robosaurus' pilot. He operates Robosaurus from a cockpit inside the mechanical beast.

MODERN MONSTERS

Nowadays monster trucks – the ones you see competing in large stadium shows – are not crudely made from the body parts of other pickups. Modern monster makers are not grease monkeys. They are professionals in white smocks. They design trucks using computers. Their goal is to create faster, safer trucks. They use lighter, stronger

WAR WIZARD

Owner:	Randy Moore
Driver:	Randy Moore
Engine:	572 custom
Home:	Bristol, Tennessee
Top speed:	112 miles per hour
Source:	www.warwizardracing.com

materials, such as steel-tube skeletons and pressurized-nitrogen shock absorbers.

WORLD'S FASTEST MONSTER TRUCK

Monster truck War Wizard, driven by Randy Moore, in 2005 went faster than 84 miles per hour on an airport runway in North Carolina to lay claim to the world's fastest monster truck, according to War Wizard's Web site.

Moore, however, claims an unofficial top speed of 112 miles per hour.

Moore beat the record previously held by BIGFOOT#14, driven by Dan Runte, who drove his monster 69.3 miles per hour in 1999.

Moore – born Dec. 17, 1963 – is the father of two daughters and a son. His hobbies include barefoot water skiing and surfing.

Moore also offers advice to kids who want to become monster truck drivers: "Set your goals, work hard and never let anyone tell you that you cannot do it!"

Moore also advises children to stay off drugs.

WORLD'S LONGEST MONSTER TRUCK JUMP

On December 19, 2009, driver Johnny Greaves set the world record by jumping the length of a football field in a Monster pickup truck. The event occurred in the foothills outside the city of San Diego, California. *The Guinness Book of World Records* calls Greaves' event, "the longest pickup truck ramp jump."

Greaves drove a monster Toyota pickup truck. His speed reached 105 miles per hour, as he hurtled down a dirt path. It sounded like a frantic bumblebee, as the truck revved

higher and higher as it climbed a dirt embankment built especially for the stunt.

It looked as if the truck had wings as it went sailing through the air and landed 301 feet away on a dirt-landing ramp. The monster jump for the new world's record was nearly 100 feet longer than the one Dan Runte had made 10 years earlier while driving BIGFOOT#14. Runte had jumped over a Boeing 727 Jetliner at an airport in Tennessee.

MONSTER FIRE TRUCK

Donald Moss, an investigator with the Virginia Beach Fire Department, used his own money to purchase a 1944 Seagrave Fire Truck, with the intent of turning it into the world's first monster fire truck. Moss sought donations from local businesses and service groups to pay for the transformation. He had the hands-on help of students from the Virginia Beach Technical and Career Education Center – who were taking welding and automotive classes there. The monster fire truck was dedicated September 15, 1995, to the city of Virginia Beach. It is used as an education tool.

"It runs on compressed natural gas," Moss said. "So it's better for the environment."

According to fire officials from Virginia Beach, there are an average of 6,000 deaths caused by

MONSTER FIRE TRUCK

Owner: Virginia Beach Fire Department
Driver/Creator: Firefighter Donald A. Moss Sr.
Style: 1944 Seagrave
Engine: 427 GMC [runs on compressed natural gas]
Home: Virginia Beach, Virginia
Source: Virginia Beach Fire Department

BLACK WIDOW

Owner: Steven Baron
Driver: Steven Baron
Style: Ford Super Duty
Engine: 502 Big Block Chevy
Home: East Haven, Connecticut
Source: www.blackwidow4x4.com

fire every year in the U.S. A quarter of those killed are children under the age of nine years old. The monster fire truck is used to get the attention of children and alert them to the dangers of fire.

THE DEADLY BLACK WIDOW

Warning: Those afraid of large spiders be warned, you are about to witness the largest Black Widow known to man.

Many years ago a monster mechanic set out on a quest to create the largest Black Widow. After years of hard work, the giant spider has been unleashed. Standing nearly 12 feet tall and 19 feet long, this giant Black Widow weighs in at 9,200 pounds. It burns methanol alcohol.

Steven Baron of East Haven, Connecticut is the owner and driver. He's been in the monster truck business for nearly two decades. You can always find Baron working on a monster truck, either his own designs or someone else's inventions. He is also on the crew for the Thrasher Monster Truck in Danbury, Connecticut.

MEGA MONSTERS

SWAMP THING THE CHANGELING

In the horror novel *Dracula*, the vampire count needs a change of scenery and – while resting in his coffin – is shipped from Transylvania to England. One may imagine the scene when the Count arrives at his destination.

I'm sure he wanted to make a good first impression. No doubt he parted his hair and brushed his fangs. Even Count Dracula can change his mailing address and cause a stir in London after midnight.

The same is true for a certain monster truck. In 2000 Dragon Slayer was also sent to England in a shipping container. Its point of origin was the United States. Out of the crate emerged Captain Insano. Two years after arriving in the UK – after a green paint job – it would become Swamp Thing.

Swamp Thing – the monster truck – is painted to look like an alligator with sharp teeth where its grill should be. It runs on methanol. It has a supercharged engine and nitro shocks. It was built in 1994 and refurbished in 2002 and 2005.

Swamp Thing's driver is Tony Dixon, a resident of Wilts, England, who became inspired in the early 1980s watching monster truck competitions on TV during Christmastime.

MEGASAURUS TO THE RESCUE!

Megasaurus, a distant mechanical relative to giant mutant monster Godzilla, is actually a former armored personnel

carrier. Top engineers converted the armored vehicle into a mechanical beast who could do battle and defeat the dinosaurs of the Jurassic Age. Megasaurus stands three stories tall and weighs 25 tons.

Megasaurus' daily diet includes automobiles, airplanes, boats and houses. He currently is on tour with some of his other souped-up friends.

A COLLISION OF MONSTER CONCEPTS

It was like attaching the legs of the Frankenstein monster to the body of a Leprechaun.

The idea of turning a Smart Car into a monster truck was hatched at a European convention in 2005 with the unveiling of the very small, diesel-powered vehicle. Only two people can fit into a Smart Car.

Stefan Attart, champion 4x4 racer from Greece, was instrumental in the transformation. He designed a Smart Car with a jacked-up DaimlerChrysler four-wheel-drive bottom. A six-cylinder diesel engine was used to power the vehicle. It has oversized wheels and a safety cage made out of aluminum tubes. The manually-controlled air springs allow the driver to adjust the angle of each tire to make it easier to go downhill.

OFF-ROAD PLACES TO TAKE YOUR MONSTER

The best place to take a monster truck for a vertical challenge is to a hill that's never been conquered. The problem with off-road driving is that steep and challenging places get to be popular – too popular. Too many monster trucks navigating over an uneven landscape will flatten it out, wrecking it for everybody.

As the old saying goes, "Too many monsters spoil the nightmare." Part of the fun of being an off-road monster is being a loner, being the first to the top. Two or three monsters may get the job done quicker, but where's the fun in that?

Many monster drivers complain fellow drivers who precede them in off-road adventures are litterbugs. Sometimes a monster truck will die on the trail. When this occurs, drivers will frequently walk away, leaving the broken down truck for scavengers to pick the monster's carcass clean. It's sort of like in the movies, after the Frankenstein monster goes berserk and wrecks his creator's laboratory. Once the monster gets beaten down, he is abandoned by the end of the film.

Don't be an irresponsible monster driver. Pick up the litter and tow away any dead monsters.

Here are five great places to go off-road with a monster pickup:

- The Grand Canyon
- The Himalayas
- The Alps
- Mount Kilimanjaro
- Machu Picchu

WHAT DO YOU NEED FOR A MONSTER JAM? TRUCKLOADS OF DIRT!

Jay Mason is the associate editor at *Mud Life* magazine. This is a magazine that reports on the virtues of driving snorting mechanical beasts into mud pits. He was behind the scenes for the setup of Monster Jam, at an event early in 2010 at Ford Field in Detroit.

He shared his experience in the April-May, 2010 edition of *Mud Life*. Mason described that the floor of the stadium was fitted with hundreds of sheets of plywood, and the first dozen rows of seats were off limits to spectators. The reason they were covered with

sheets of plastic is to make cleanup easier.

What impressed Mason most were the mountains of dirt trucked into the stadium.

According to Mason, truckload after truckload of dirt came in and began to pile up as the work crews started to spread it across the playing field. A local towing company supplied the cars that were to be crushed. They were brought in as the dirt was being spread around.

"Imagine a large pile of ants scurrying around, attacking a melting popsicle lying on summertime concrete," Mason wrote. "Now imagine [that] all the ants were the size of 50-ton Caterpillar loaders. Yeah. Wow!"

IN CANADA IT'S KNOWN AS MONSTER SPECTACULAR

Hockey is not the only thing that will send a Canadian's blood pressure skyrocketing.

Doug de Nance, a blogger and the voice of Canada's Monster Spectacular, is an excitable fellow who turns beet red as he hollers into public address systems, describing the action at monster shows. He wrote about the start of the Monster Spectacular tour:

"As a freak spring snowstorm blasted across the soon-to-be wheat fields of Saskatchewan, Monster Spectacular stormed into the provincial capital for the second stop of the 2010 Canadian tour. While the cold winds blew outside Regina's Brandt Centre, the competition heated up inside with teammate rivalries."

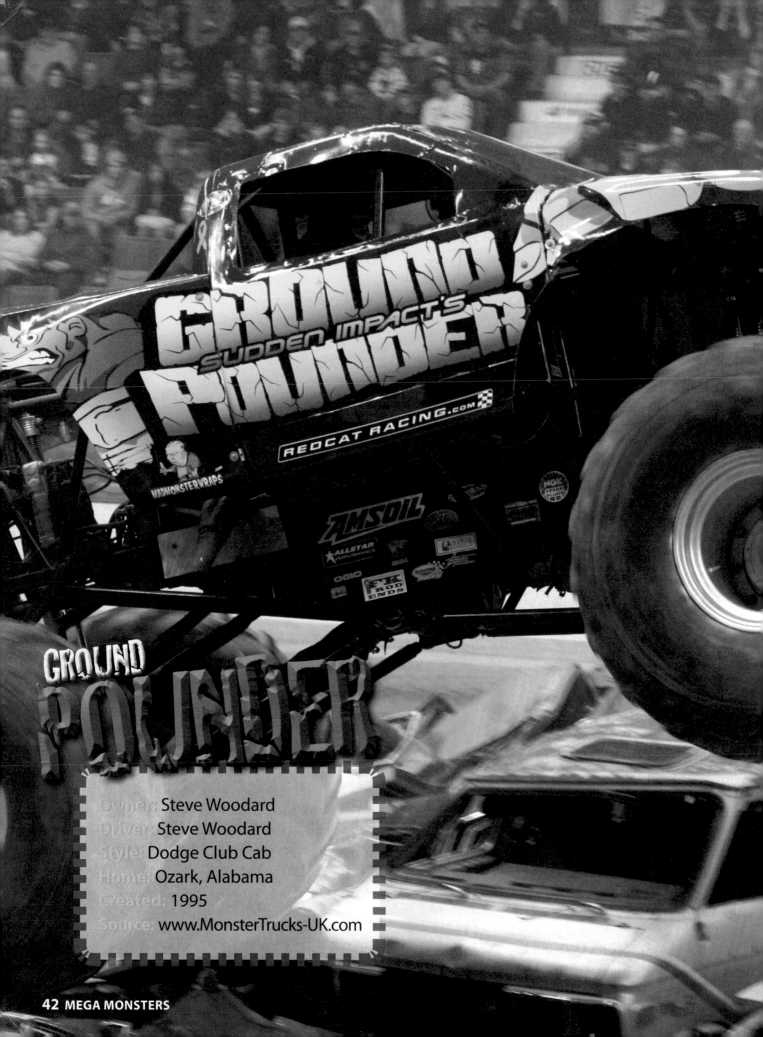

GROUND POUNDER

Owner: Steve Woodard
Driver: Steve Woodard
Style: Dodge Club Cab
Home: Ozark, Alabama
Created: 1995
Source: www.MonsterTrucks-UK.com

A week prior, he wrote about 50,000 fans at Olympic Stadium in Montreal for the start of the Monster Spectacular 2010 tour, which he compared to the launching of a rocket.

"Typically the first monster truck event is a wheelie contest," he wrote. "But this time things got really big – as in 'big air.' It was a monster truck long-jump contest. … It truly was a 'blast off' as they headed into orbit, jumping well over 80 feet. The truck everybody was gunning for used all of the 1,800 horsepower Bounty Hunter had to give to win with a monster long jump of 93 feet."

THE SMACK ON TED SMAK, MASTER MONSTER BUILDER

Ted Smak – whose last name is pronounced "smack!" – has a monster factory near Chicago, Illinois. He has been in business since 1983 and makes an

average of about 500 monsters a year. Smak has everything you need to complete your perfect specimen from rooftop spotlights all the way down to the steering knuckles. Drivers can drop in and pick up the parts needed to convert a vehicle into a monster, take the parts home and do it themselves, or they let Smak do the job for them. The cost of making a monster starts at $3,500, but could cost as much as $20,000.

Smak calls the monster trucks, his "big toys." His shop is so popular that it is open seven days a week. It is always busy, even on Sundays.

"How do you make a monster truck?" Smak asks. "You jack up the suspension on a Jeep or pickup and put on big wheels. A roll bar is nice, but you can't really call it a monster without the big wheels."

Street monsters are a lot different from the kind of monster trucks you'll see at big stadium shows. It is against the law to drive a stadium-sized monster on a public street. Besides scaring other motorists, it can be unsafe. A monster can roll over easily because its center of gravity has been hoisted in the air. Plus, a stadium monster is extra tall. Imagine Grave Digger, the giant truck featured on the Monster Jam circuit, snorting and rolling down Main Street. And you wouldn't want BIGFOOT 5 to pull up next to you at a stoplight. It has Army-surplus Firestone tires, which are 10-feet tall. BIGFOOT 5 is the biggest monster truck of all time and is parked in front of Bob Chandler's place – BIGFOOT 4X4 Inc., in Hazelwood, Missouri.

Smak said he's been to Chandler's house in St. Louis on several occasions and has bought

BIGFOOT

Owner: Bob Chandler
Drivers: Dan Runte, Rick Long, Ron Bachman, Rodney Tweedy, Nigel Morris, Alan Hartsock, Eric Meagher, Keith Sturgeon, Jerry Dalton , Brian Bertoletti & Madusa
Style: Ford Pickup
Engine: 572 Ford Hemi
Home: Hazelwood, Missouri
Created: 1975
Source: www.offroaders.com

parts from Chandler. He was the top bidder at an auction for BIGFOOT's tailgate, the first monster truck in recorded history. The tailgate is currently hanging in Smak's shop, in deference to the creator of the monster truck phenomenon.

SUPER FAN

Andrew Fielder, a chef from England, became monster-struck when he saw his first junk cars run over and crushed on a television show in 1985. In 1993 Fielder went to see BIGFOOT 6 when it was touring the United Kingdom. He brought his camera and snapped pictures of the car-crushing event.

"A couple of years later, when I first got onto the Internet, I found there were very few Web sites with monster trucks … I decided to make a Web site of my own," Fielder writes on the Web site that he created in 1996.

He said for a few years all he had were just the few photographs of BIGFOOT 6 posted on his Web site. Fielder started vacationing in the U.S. so he could see monster truck

shows and rub elbows with the top drivers. He moved to the United States in 1999. He got to be friends with many monster truck drivers and photographed assorted acts of destruction.

In August 2009 Fielder sold his Web site, but it is still live today. You can visit it at www.MonsterTrucks-UK.com, and see photographs of some of your favorite monsters, including BIGFOOT, the Executioner and Grave Digger.